Lerner SPORTS

SUPER SPORTS
TEAMS

INSIDE THE
PITTSBURGH
STEELERS

CHRISTINA HILL

Lerner Publications ◆ Minneapolis

SPORTS THRILLS *MEET* RESEARCH SKILLS

Lerner | SPORTS

Free Database Trial: **lernersports.com**

Copyright © 2023 by Lerner Publishing Group, Inc.

All rights reserved. International copyright secured. No part of this book may be reproduced, stored in a retrieval system, or transmitted in any form or by any means—electronic, mechanical, photocopying, recording, or otherwise—without the prior written permission of Lerner Publishing Group, Inc., except for the inclusion of brief quotations in an acknowledged review.

Lerner Publications Company
An imprint of Lerner Publishing Group, Inc.
241 First Avenue North
Minneapolis, MN 55401 USA

For reading levels and more information, look up this title at www.lernerbooks.com.

Main body text set in Aptifer Slab LT Pro / Typeface provided by Linotype AG

Library of Congress Cataloging-in-Publication Data
Names: Hill, Christina, author.
Title: Inside the Pittsburgh Steelers / Christina Hill.
Other titles: Steelers
Description: Minneapolis, MN : Lerner Publications, [2023] | Series: Super Sports Teams (Lerner Sports) | Includes bibliographical references and index. | Audience: Ages 7–11 years | Audience: Grades 2–3 | Summary: "The Pittsburgh Steelers are a legendary NFL team. Their six Super Bowl wins are tied for the most in league history. Read about the team's history, great players, and plans for winning another Super Bowl"— Provided by publisher.
Identifiers: LCCN 2021058559 (print) | LCCN 2021058560 (ebook) | ISBN 9781728458106 (Library Binding) | ISBN 9781728463438 (Paperback) | ISBN 9781728462387 (eBook)
Subjects: LCSH: Pittsburgh Steelers (Football team)—History—Juvenile literature. | Football players—Pennsylvania—Pittsburgh—History—Juvenile literature. | Football—Pennsylvania—Pittsburgh—History—Juvenile literature.
Classification: LCC GV956.P57 H55 2023 (print) | LCC GV956.P57 (ebook) | DDC 796.332/640974886—dc23/eng/20220114

LC record available at https://lccn.loc.gov/2021058559
LC ebook record available at https://lccn.loc.gov/2021058560

Manufactured in the United States of America
1 – CG – 7/15/22

TABLE OF CONTENTS

Pittsburgh Steelers defender "Mean" Joe Greene (*left*) got his nickname from his college football team, the North Texas Mean Green.

LEGENDARY PLAY

FACTS AT A GLANCE

- The Pittsburgh Steelers were originally the **PITTSBURGH PIRATES**.

- The Steelers won the **SUPER BOWL** in 1975, 1976, 1979, 1980, 2006, and 2009.

- The **STEELERS** are the only team that has won back-to-back Super Bowls twice.

- The **ROONEY** family has owned the team since it started.

- At the age of 23, **BEN ROETHLISBERGER** became the youngest quarterback to win a Super Bowl.

In 1972, the Pittsburgh Steelers earned their first American Football Conference (AFC) Central Division title. They had a chance to make a run to the Super Bowl. But first, they would have to face a tough Oakland Raiders team. The Steelers had a slight edge for the season with 11 wins. The Raiders had 10 wins.

At halftime, the score was still 0–0. Then the Steelers scored six points on two field goals. But the Raiders turned the game around with a fourth-quarter touchdown. With 22 seconds remaining, the

Steelers were down 7–6. They had the ball on their own 40-yard line. What happened next was one of the most exciting plays in National Football League (NFL) history.

Raiders players were closing in on Pittsburgh quarterback Terry Bradshaw. He quickly threw the ball deep down the field to running back John Fuqua. But as the football sailed through the air, Fuqua and Raiders player Jack Tatum collided. Neither player caught the ball as it bounced away from them. Many fans thought this was the end of the play. But it wasn't over yet.

Pro Football Hall of Famer Terry Bradshaw played in the NFL for 14 seasons.

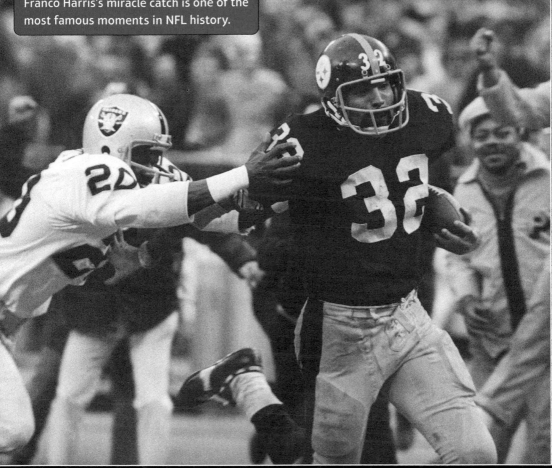

Franco Harris's miracle catch is one of the most famous moments in NFL history.

After the football bounced off Fuqua or Tatum, it flew right to Steelers running back Franco Harris. Harris scooped up the ball before it touched the ground. He ran into the end zone for a game-winning touchdown. The stadium erupted in cheers.

The Steelers won the game 13–7. They moved on to the AFC Championship but lost to the Miami Dolphins. Pittsburgh's season was over. But Steelers fans will never forget the 1972 season or Harris's game-winning touchdown.

Bill Cowher was an NFL
linebacker for four seasons
before becoming Pittsburgh's
coach in 1992.

STEELER NATION

For Arthur J. Rooney, sports were everything. He wanted to start a pro football team in Pittsburgh, Pennsylvania. However, the state laws did not allow pro sports on Sundays, when most NFL games take place.

In 1933, the state laws changed, and Rooney started the Pittsburgh Pirates. He named his team after the Major League Baseball (MLB) team of the same name. The Rooney family has owned the franchise ever since.

This statue of Arthur J. Rooney sits outside Heinz Field, the home stadium of the Steelers. The statue weighs more than 80 tons (72 t).

At first, Rooney's team struggled to win games. In 1940, he decided to hold a contest to rename the team. Fans voted and chose the Pittsburgh Steelers. The name honors the city's steel production. Rooney wanted his team to be closely linked to Pittsburgh, and the name *Steelers* was the perfect way to celebrate the city.

From 1933 to 1968, the Steelers went through 13 different coaches. Then the franchise hired Chuck Noll in 1969. Noll coached the Steelers to many wins in his 23 years with the team, including four Super Bowls.

Chuck Noll (*left*) won 209 games with the Steelers. Noll and quarterback Terry Bradshaw (*right*) led the Steelers to four Super Bowl wins.

Pittsburgh International Airport is famous for its statue of Franco Harris (*pictured*). The statue shows Harris's amazing catch from the 1972 game against the Raiders.

When Noll retired, Bill Cowher took over. Coaching from 1992 to 2006, Cowher led the team to their fifth Super Bowl win in 2006. In 2007, Mike Tomlin became head coach and took the team to yet another Super Bowl win in 2009.

The Steelers won 13 playoff games at Three Rivers Stadium.

Steelers fans support their team in good times and bad. These loyal fans are nicknamed the Steeler Nation. The Steelers have sold out every home game since 1972.

When the steel industry in Pittsburgh declined in the 1970s, many workers had to leave the city in search of new jobs. But many of them remained Steelers fans. The Steelers are often called the Black and Gold because of their uniform colors, which come from the city flag. Fans wearing black and gold help fill NFL stadiums across the country.

In their early years, the Steelers shared Forbes Field with MLB's Pittsburgh Pirates. Then from 1964 to 1969, they played at Pitt Stadium where the University of Pittsburgh Panthers played. In 1970, the Steelers and the Pirates moved into Three Rivers Stadium. Finally, in 2001, the Steelers moved into brand-new Heinz Field. They share the stadium with the Panthers college football team. Heinz Field is shaped like a horseshoe. It has the Allegheny River on one side and the Pittsburgh skyline on the other.

The Steelers have sold out every home game at Heinz Field, which seats 68,400 fans.

Quarterback Ben Roethlisberger has been to the Pro Bowl six times. The Pro Bowl is the NFL's all-star game.

AMAZING MOMENTS

The Steelers began to dominate the NFL in the 1970s under Coach Noll's leadership. Led by quarterback Terry Bradshaw and the Steel Curtain defense, the team faced the Minnesota Vikings in the 1975 Super Bowl. The Vikings also had a strong defense, so both teams struggled to score. But the Steelers were determined to win. The Vikings could only score six points, and it wasn't enough. The Steelers won their first Super Bowl 16–6.

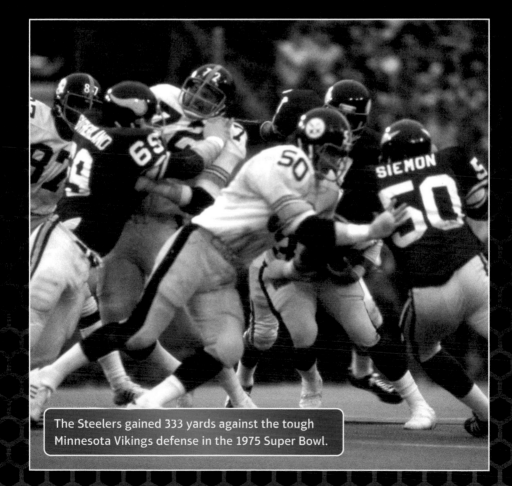

The Steelers gained 333 yards against the tough Minnesota Vikings defense in the 1975 Super Bowl.

The Steelers returned to the Super Bowl the following year. They faced the Dallas Cowboys. Bradshaw threw a 53-yard pass to wide receiver Lynn Swann, who jumped high in the air to catch it. But a Dallas player also tried to grab the ball. The two players juggled the football back and forth until Swann finally secured it. That moment is one of the most incredible catches in NFL history. The Steelers took home their second Super Bowl title by winning the game 21–17.

The Steelers continued their winning streak. They won their third and fourth Super Bowls in back-to-back years in 1979 and 1980. In the 1990s, the Steelers won five AFC Central Division titles. They returned to the Super Bowl in 1996 but lost to the Cowboys.

Hines Ward played 14 seasons with the Steelers and had 12,083 career receiving yards.

In 2006, the Steelers played in the Super Bowl yet again. They faced the Seattle Seahawks. Steelers running back Willie Parker had an amazing 75-yard touchdown run in the third quarter. The Steelers led 14–3. Then Steelers wide receiver Antwaan Randle El surprised everyone by throwing a 43-yard touchdown pass to Hines Ward. The Steelers won 21–10.

STEELERS FACT

The Steelers are tied with the New England Patriots for the most Super Bowl wins with six.

The latest Super Bowl win for the Steelers was in 2009 against the Arizona Cardinals. The Steelers were down by three points with only 42 seconds left in the game. But then quarterback Ben Roethlisberger and wide receiver Santonio Holmes pulled off a great play. Roethlisberger threw the ball into the end zone and managed to avoid three Cardinals defenders. With perfect timing, Holmes jumped high into the air and caught the ball. He landed with his toes barely inside the corner of the end zone, giving Pittsburgh the win 27–23.

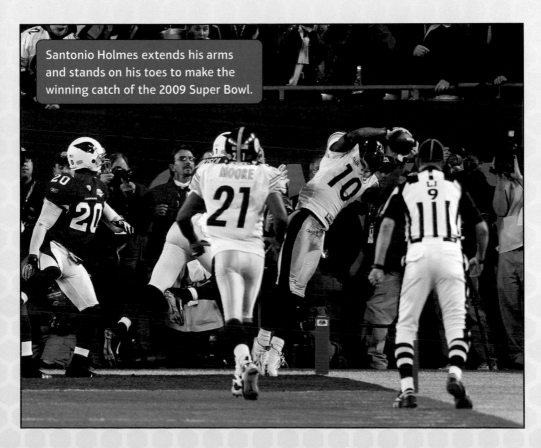

Santonio Holmes extends his arms and stands on his toes to make the winning catch of the 2009 Super Bowl.

After his successful NFL career ended, Terry Bradshaw became a sports broadcaster.

STEELERS SUPERSTARS

The Steelers have a long list of superstar players and coaches who have led the franchise to greatness. Behind every great team is a great leader, and the Steelers found theirs in 1969 with coach Chuck Noll. The Steelers had the worst record in the NFL when Noll was hired. He quickly turned things around by drafting star players. He created an unstoppable defense nicknamed the Steel Curtain.

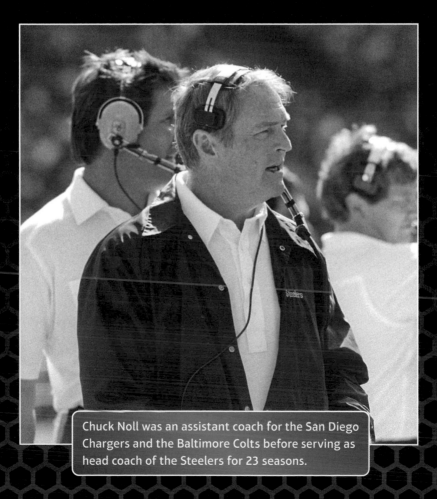

Chuck Noll was an assistant coach for the San Diego Chargers and the Baltimore Colts before serving as head coach of the Steelers for 23 seasons.

Defender "Mean" Joe Greene led the Steel Curtain defense. He is one of the best players in Steelers history. Greene won the NFL Rookie of the Year award in 1969. He was the first player to catch an interception, force a fumble, and recover a fumble in a Super Bowl game. Greene won NFL Defensive Player of the Year in 1972 and 1974.

The Steelers drafted Terry Bradshaw in 1970. Bradshaw was the first quarterback in NFL history to win four Super Bowls. He won the Super Bowl Most Valuable Player award twice. He retired in 1983 and began a career as a sports broadcaster.

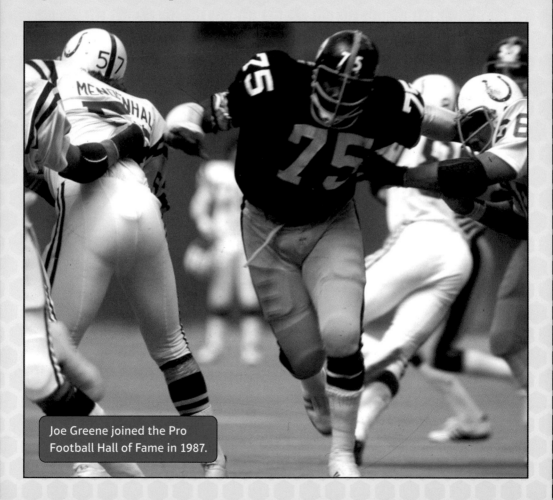

Joe Greene joined the Pro Football Hall of Fame in 1987.

STEELERS FACT

The Steelers have 32 former players and coaches in the Pro Football Hall of Fame.

Ben Roethlisberger wears number 7 to honor his favorite player, quarterback John Elway.

The Steelers chose Ben Roethlisberger in the first round of the 2004 NFL Draft. Nicknamed Big Ben, he became the youngest quarterback to win the Super Bowl at 23. Roethlisberger leads the Steelers in passing attempts, pass completions, yards, and touchdowns.

Linebacker T. J. Watt joined the Steelers in 2017. He came from a football family, with two older brothers also playing in the NFL. Watt showed how good he was in his first NFL game against the Cleveland Browns. He recorded seven tackles, two sacks, and one interception.

T. J. Watt was the Steelers sack leader from 2019 through 2021.

In 2021, the Steelers drafted running back Najee Harris in the first round. Harris is already setting records that prove the Steelers made a smart choice. He had an amazing game against the Denver Broncos in his first year. Harris recorded 122 yards and a touchdown, helping the Steelers win 27–19.

Running back Najee Harris jumps over a defender to avoid being tackled.

Steelers fans love to cheer on their team.

HERE WE GO, STEELERS!

The Steelers are one of the most successful NFL teams. They have a long history of greatness on the field. Fans are loyal because the team always works hard to win.

Steelers fans are easy to spot at games because they are often waving Terrible Towels. Terrible Towels are simple yellow towels with black text that reads, "The Terrible Towel: A Pittsburgh Original." Steelers fans love to wave them at games and other places. Fans take photos of the towels all around the world. Terrible Towels have even been to space! Astronauts Mike Fincke and Drew Morgan took Terrible Towels on missions to the International Space Station.

The Steelers give some of the money they make from selling Terrible Towels to a local charity.

Coach Mike Tomlin has drafted a new round of superstar players who are sure to keep Steeler Nation cheering. Longtime quarterback Roethlisberger will soon retire, so the team will try to find a new leader for the offense. But no matter who plays quarterback, the famous Steelers defense will help the team win games. Led by defenders Cam Heyward and T. J. Watt, the Steelers and Steeler Nation are ready to win another Super Bowl.

Cam Heyward led the Steelers with 12 sacks in the 2017 season.

STEELERS FACT

The Steelers are the only NFL team that have logos on only one side of their helmets.

At 36, Mike Tomlin was the youngest coach to ever win a Super Bowl when the Steelers beat the Cardinals in 2009.

Former Steelers running back Jerome Bettis earned the nickname The Bus for his size and strength.

STEELERS
SEASON RECORD HOLDERS

RUSHING TOUCHDOWNS

1. Franco Harris, 14 (1976)
2. Jerome Bettis, 13 (2004)
   Willie Parker, 13 (2006)
   Rashard Mendenhall, 13 (2010)
3. James Conner, 12 (2018)

RECEIVING TOUCHDOWNS

1. Antonio Brown, 15 (2018)
2. Antonio Brown, 13 (2014)
3. Louis Lipps, 12 (1985)
   Hines Ward, 12 (2002)
   Antonio Brown, 12 (2016)

PASSING YARDS

1. Ben Roethlisberger, 5,129 (2018)
2. Ben Roethlisberger, 4,952 (2014)
3. Ben Roethlisberger, 4,328 (2009)
4. Ben Roethlisberger, 4,261 (2013)
5. Ben Roethlisberger, 4,251 (2017)

RUSHING YARDS

1. Barry Foster, 1,690 (1992)
2. Jerome Bettis, 1,665 (1997)
3. Willie Parker, 1,494 (2006)
4. Jerome Bettis, 1,431 (1996)
5. Le'Veon Bell, 1,361 (2014)

PASS CATCHES

1. Antonio Brown, 136 (2015)
2. Antonio Brown, 129 (2014)
3. Hines Ward, 112 (2002)
4. JuJu Smith-Schuster, 111 (2018)
5. Antonio Brown, 110 (2013)

SACKS

1. T. J. Watt, 22.5 (2021)
2. James Harrison, 16.0 (2008)
3. Mike Merriweather, 15.0 (1984)
   T. J. Watt, 15.0 (2020)
4. T. J. Watt, 14.5 (2019)

GLOSSARY

American Football Conference (AFC): with the National Football Conference, one of the two groups of teams that make up the NFL

draft: to choose new players for a sports team

end zone: the area at each end of a football field where players score touchdowns

field goal: a score of three points in football made by kicking the ball over the crossbar

franchise: a team that is a member of a professional sports league

fumble: when a football player loses hold of the ball while handling or running with it

interception: a pass caught by the defending team

linebacker: a defender who usually plays in the middle of the defense

pro: short for *professional*, taking part in an activity for money

rookie: a first-year player in a sport

sports broadcaster: a person who talks about sports on a TV, radio, or internet show